Dr Barnardo

by

Laurie Sheehan

First published in 2001
by Anglia Young Books
Anglia Young Books is an imprint of
MILL PUBLISHING
PO Box 55
4 Balloo Avenue
Bangor
Co. Down BT19 7PJ

reprinted 2008

Illustrations by Robin Lawrie

British Library Cataloguing-in-Publication Data

A catalogue record for this book is available
from the British Library

ISBN 1871173 68 X

Printed in Great Britain by Ashford Colour Press,
Gosport, Hampshire

Dr Barnardo

Author's Note

Thomas Barnardo gave homes to 60,000 waifs and created Britain's biggest children's charity. Today the charity's slogan is, 'Giving children back their future'. Barnardo's deals with children in the most difficult circumstances and works to stop childhood problems leading to an unhappy adulthood. Dr Barnardo believed that caring for children in the community, and not in an institution, prepared them better for living in the real world. The people now in charge agree with this and the charity no longer runs orphanages. Instead, children live with families or in council homes. But Barnardo's does help over 55,000 youngsters and their families each year in over 300 services in the UK. There are independent Barnardo organizations in the Irish Republic, Australia and New Zealand.

Barnardo's life has been so well recorded that we know what he said. In just a few cases, to enliven the narrative, I have imagined what he may have said. He romanticized some details of earlier events, like his contacts with, and influence on, Lord Shaftesbury. His achievements were monumental enough without needing fictitious additions. *The Manchester Evening Chronicle* said, 'He has left behind him such an enduring monument to noble self-

sacrificing effort, such a legacy of good deeds well done, such a claim upon the reverence of the nation as few men among us will leave.'

There have been a number of books on Barnardo since Syrie Barnardo and James Marchant wrote their *Memoirs of the late Dr Barnardo* (1907). I am particularly indebted to his secretary A.E. Williams's *Barnardo of Stepney*, Gillian Wagner's *Barnardo* and June Rose's *For the Sake of the Children*.

Chapter One

Tom Barnardo was born in Dublin on 4 July 1845 and no-one expected him to live. His mother was too weak to nurse him so he was cared for by his half-sister, Sophie, who was seventeen.

Tom was the eighth surviving child of John Michaelis Barnardo, who sold furs to the rich folk of Dublin. The family lived in a five-storeyed house in fashionable Dame Street and John Barnardo had a shop below the house.

At that time, there was great poverty in Ireland. But soon things were made worse by famine, because a disease had destroyed the potato crop, the only food grown by the common people. By 1847, the Irish were dying in their tens of thousands.

Tom himself caught diphtheria, a disease affecting the throat and air passages. Week after week he fought for life but, finally, he was declared dead by two doctors. However, just as the undertakers were lifting his body into his coffin, his heart gave a slight flutter. Then it fluttered again. Instead of being buried alive, Tom Barnardo would live to fight another day!

Tom was a small, plain, sickly child but his younger brother, Henry, was good-looking and charming and he also had a good singing voice. Everyone loved Henry and he was often asked to entertain visitors who would reward him with chocolates, which he never shared.

Finally Tom could take no more and he hit out at Henry in a jealous rage: 'That's for showing off with your singing,' he roared, thumping the sticky-mouthed Henry in the

chest when he returned to the nursery with an empty chocolate-box. 'And that,' he continued, pushing him against the rocking-horse, 'is for not even saving me one chocolate. You pig! You horrible pig!'

But Sophie was his friend. Other boys of his age started school but Tom was still small and often seriously ill, so Sophie became his teacher. A quick, bright boy, he soon learnt to read and write and, when he was strong enough, he went to St Ann's Sunday School, run by Dean Dickinson and his curate, Mr Sanders. Tom liked the way these kind and religious men treated him: no shouting, no bullying, just quiet orderliness. So, at least for an hour every week, Tom was well behaved.

This all changed when he went to his first day school, St John's. He was very naughty and gave his teacher no end of trouble. Tom was ten now and he was showing his true character. Nobody was going to tell *him* what to do.

He'd thought that St John's was bad enough. But when he followed two of his brothers, George and Fred, as a pupil at St

Patrick's Cathedral Grammar School, he realized how lucky he'd been.

The Principal, the Reverend William Dundas, took a savage delight in beating some of the boys. Luckily Tom was not one of them, even though he was always talking. He misbehaved because he was bored, having learnt his lessons quickly. After the lessons, came games practice, which he dreaded, being the smallest boy. He was good at swimming, though.

Towards the end of his schooldays, he hated sports even more. He was now wearing thick blue-tinted spectacles because he was so short-sighted. 'All I want to do is read my books, not play games!' he raged. But, unfortunately, though the books he read were interesting, they weren't the right ones to help him pass exams. He hated exams. 'Nobody has the right to judge Tom Barnardo!' he claimed.

So, at sixteen, having failed his exams, he was apprenticed to a wine merchant.

At about this time, Tom's mother and George and Fred began going to religious meetings in the Metropolitan Hall, Abbey

Street. These 'Revival' meetings had spread from America. Excited preachers called Evangelicals urged sinners to mend their ways.

The preachers kept talking about death and damnation. Death was an everyday event in this city of the poor, the diseased and the starving, and the Evangelicals' message struck a chord with many Dubliners. But Tom's father was unimpressed by all this 'ranting'; he was now supplying furs to the court and, in court circles, such meetings were not fashionable.

Tom, too, was mixing with the rich, selling them wine for their parties and balls. He had become fashionable himself, dressing smartly, buying the finest suits and wearing spotless white shirts, smart gloves and a silk hat.

But Tom's mother was always asking him to come along to the revivalist meetings and, to please her, he reluctantly went. He thought that the crowds were all mad, though.

Slowly, however, Tom changed his mind about the Evangelicals. It didn't happen overnight; it happened gradually, when he started to attend meetings in ordinary homes, away from the hysterical crowds. It was here, where the message of Christ's love and salvation was a simple one delivered by caring and dedicated people, that the whole thing began to make sense to him.

His conviction grew and grew and, by the spring of 1862, Tom decided to dedicate his life to Christ and to carrying out His teachings. He got permission to teach a Bible class on Sunday mornings at a 'ragged school' for stinking, lice-infested urchins.

Tom was still very small (he'd only grown to five foot three) and his tinted spectacles gave him an odd, vacant expression, but he braved the ruffians of Dublin's most dangerous area to visit his pupils' jobless and sick parents in the overcrowded, narrow alleys of 'the Liberties'. Under his arm was a small leather case containing religious pamphlets and also packets of tea for the elderly.

Many a flimsy door was slammed in his face but he persevered among the decaying hovels which were so different from his own Georgian house.

Tom made a vow: 'I must do something

to save these ignorant, whiskey-drinking slum-dwellers so they'll go to heaven one day.'

Tom had no patience with the Church of Ireland, even though he'd been confirmed by the Archbishop of Dublin. Old bishops were too slow and bossy for this inspired young man of seventeen. Folk needed to be told now, in an exciting way, about God's Word.

So Tom left the Church of Ireland and joined the Plymouth Brethren, an Evangelical movement, who did not believe in bishops. Nobody was going to tell the Brethren what to do - or Tom! They also believed that if they devoted their lives to preaching about Jesus, they should be supported by voluntary contributions, so Tom became a Sunday school teacher and worker at their Merrion Hall centre.

Tom joined the Swift's Alley Mission, too. One day, he was walking from hovel to hovel down the long, winding Marrowbone Lane in the Liberties. With him was Mr Richard Owens who was training him in these home visits, where they read and prayed with the poor and delivered religious leaflets. 'Mr Owens, why do you have a walking-stick?' asked Tom. 'Habit,' replied Owens. 'I always like a cane or umbrella in my hand.' 'So did I,' said Tom, 'but I had to give it up because one day these boys so annoyed me, gathering round me in the street, that I lost patience. It was all I could do to keep myself from striking them with the walking-stick. If I had, it would have killed my work for the Lord.'

They reached the end of the lane. Here was the widows' alms-house, where Tom always delighted the poverty-stricken women with his gifts of tea. More than a million people had died during the five years of famine in Ireland; few had ever tasted tea.

Chapter Two

But Tom Barnardo was restless. He was desperate to spread the Word of God in other countries.

On a cold February evening in 1866, the twenty-year-old Tom went to hear the founder of the China Inland Mission, Dr Hudson Taylor, address a room full of enthusiastic young men.

'A million a month are dying in China without knowing Christ,' declared Dr Hudson Taylor. The good doctor was even shorter than Tom. Tom whispered to his neighbour, 'There's hope for me!'

Tom and three others volunteered to be missionaries. Hudson said that he was returning to China at the end of May. If they wished to join him, they must go to London to catch the ship. Tom was so excited, he later wrote a poem, 'God's Call to China'.

Tom's father thought that it was a stupid idea and refused to help him with money but three Brethren elders gave Tom a small sum to tide him over in London, where he and his new friends would join other China candidates.

So Tom and the others went to London - 'a huge, bustling, noisy, stinking place!' - where they stayed at a lodging-house in Stepney.

But Tom's excitement was short-lived. Six weeks later, on a May morning, he was thoroughly dejected. He was down at the docks, saying goodbye to his friends. Everyone, except Tom, was sailing to China with Hudson. The little man had told Tom, 'Before you become a missionary, you need to grow more: not in size but in maturity. We cannot have a missionary who has peculiar beliefs, the intensity of which makes him unable to take orders or even advice. You're talented but so overbearing. I'm sure you'd sorely try even some of our most patient labourers in Christ. I was amused by your many criticisms of the way I run the Mission; some of my people were not.'

It was a bitter pill to swallow and, for some time, Tom smarted with resentment but, in the end, he decided to take Hudson's advice and begin medical studies. If he became a doctor, he could at least earn a living whether he went to China or not.

He found new lodgings: two rooms in a quiet street behind the London Hospital, where Hudson himself had trained. Tom was hoping to register at the hospital's medical college.

On Friday the 13th of July, a cholera patient was rushed to the hospital and this dangerous infection was soon sweeping through the East End of London. Each dark, stinking, disease-ridden hovel was filled with several large families, their dogs and some-times their pigs and donkeys, too. 'No wonder there's cholera, with all this overcrowding and no sanitation!' cried Tom.

The East End was overflowing not just with filth but with country folk and foreign and Irish immigrants. They were looking for work when there was so much unemployment already. London's population had doubled in thirty years. The new railways had not helped the housing shortage; lines now ran where thousands of people used to live.

Every morning, Tom was woken by the clatter of horses' hoofs on the cobbles. Pickford's removal vans were taking away the dead from the hospital for burial in shallow mass graves in the reeking, over-full burial grounds. The London Hospital only had three hundred beds and it could not cope. So hundreds of the sick had to stay at home; people who were well at dawn were dead by dusk.

Though Tom was not yet a medical student, he bravely visited the homes of the sick and dying. He comforted men, women and children as they lay vomiting and screaming and writhing with severe cramps. He prayed with them as they died. One terrible day, he saw sixteen die. Cholera killed nearly four thousand East Enders in three months.

At last, though, he began studying at the London Hospital's modern medical college but also found time to preach with the Sidney Street Brethren. One day, passing the college smoking-room, he overheard some students talking. 'Queer fellow Barnardo. Seems to me he's got something on his mind. He's up to something we don't know of. Is there a woman?' 'Rot,' said another student. 'A fellow told me he saw him in the street preaching yesterday evening.' Then everyone shouted, 'Preaching! A religious crank! Let's drop him!'

He never told them that he'd heard but he knew that he was the odd one out, never going to student parties or attending the theatre, so he had few friends among the students. But his religious fervour was undimmed and now he decided to work with children in the Stepney slums.

Tom found a Sunday Ragged School in Ernest Street, one of the toughest parts of Stepney. He became an unpaid teacher to what he called 'a rough crowd' of young people under twenty-eight and 'disordered children'. A third of the pupils had been in jail. Over a hundred were packed into a low, narrow, badly ventilated room, seating only eighty-six. In summer, it was often so stifling that they had to rush outside for air, but Tom endured this, just as he endured the pupils' taunting.

One Sunday, some of the older fellows bundled him out of the window. Luckily it was a single-storey building and only his dignity was hurt. 'Turn the other cheek, man. Turn the other cheek,' he muttered to himself as the grinning devils slammed down the window. Mr Barnardo found his unbroken spectacles, picked himself up, brushed off the dust and made a dignified return. He continued with the lesson as if nothing had happened. The whole class was astonished. How unruffled he was! There was even a twinkle in those eyes peering over the glasses.

Soon Tom had won them over. He'd achieved it by his sympathy, his sincere efforts to understand them, and the increasing liveliness of his humour. And especially by his enthusiasm and ability to make his lessons

interesting. He became so good at his job that he was soon promoted to superintendent. He was now having to turn away two hundred young people every week

Tom had a letter published in *The Revival*, an Evangelical journal. He appealed for £200 from the public. He said that the youngsters' needs could not be met by Ernest Street because money matters were handled by a committee, who were unable to raise enough. He needed to obtain a building seating six hundred and the voluntary help of fifty Evangelicals. To get things started, he wanted to hold a large 'tea-meeting'. 'Free tea and buns,' he thought, 'accompanied by the Word of Life from Tom Barnardo. What more could any young person want?'

The committee members were angry, feeling that their school's success was being used as a means to raise money for another school. And the arrogant Barnardo had not even asked their permission! The quarrel led to his resignation. But he did receive £90 from the public. He also had an offer to use the Assembly Rooms over the King's Arms, Mile End Road, for his free teas. 'I'll use the

Press again!' he vowed.

On Sunday 5 November 1867, Tom and a few friends provided tea and buns for 2,347 children. Many of the older ones were thieves and street girls. They loved the tea and buns but Tom's preaching was drowned by the din. On the seventh Sunday, a new landlord banned the event; Tom's free food might draw customers away from the bar!

The money had been spent but the fight must go on. Tom persuaded three fellow medical students to rent an old donkey-shed with him and to share the teaching. On the first Sunday, a crowd of urchins filled the place as soon as Tom opened the doors. He planned to open two evenings a week, too. But the venture did not last long, because he was exhausted. He had worn himself out and he suffered a nervous collapse.

But by 2 March 1868, he was well enough to open the East End Juvenile Mission. It was in Hope Place, a blind alley surrounded by little single-storey houses. With his friends' help, he rented two four-roomed cottages and by knocking the four rooms into one, he made a schoolroom in each cottage: a boys' school and a girls' school. There'd be no shortage of pupils. Tom was back studying hard at the college; he would be teaching for just two evenings a week and on Sundays. If he stayed well.

Chapter Three

It was a winter's evening two years later. Tom and his helpers were about to turn out the gas-lights in the boys' school and go home. Then they noticed a skinny little straw-haired lad huddled by the large fire. It was half-past nine and an icy wind was blowing outside. Wearing neither shirt, shoes nor stockings, the child was shivering violently. He looked far poorer than any of the other pupils. His body was that of a seven-year-old child but his grimy face was careworn, like an old man's.

'Come, my lad,' said Tom, kindly, 'hadn't you better get home? It's very late.' The boy twisted his tattered cap in his hands. 'Please, sir,' he said slowly, 'let me stop.' 'No, I can't,' said Tom, yawning. 'Your mother will wonder what's kept you so late.' The boy scratched his louse-ridden head. 'I ain't got no mother.' Tom frowned. 'Haven't got a mother, boy? Where do you live?' 'I don't live nowhere,' whispered the boy. Tom frowned again, 'Now, my lad, it's no good your trying to deceive me. Where do you come from? Where did you sleep last night?' The boy hung his head. 'In Whitechapel, along the Haymarket in one of them carts filled with hay. Then I met a chap I knew and he told me to come here. He said perhaps you'd let me lie near the fire all night. I won't do no harm if you let me stop.'

Tom was shocked. 'Are there many such as you?' 'Oh yes, sir, lots, heaps of us! More than I could count!'

Although Tom was exhausted, he was determined to see these homeless children for himself. 'Now, lad,' he said, 'if I'm willing to give you some hot coffee and some food and a place to sleep in, will you take me to where some of those poor boys are?'

With their heads bowed against the biting wind, Tom and the boy battled their way to Tom's lodgings. He lit the gas-lamp and a big fire. Then they sat at the table beside the blaze and sipped the hot, sweet coffee. Tom gave the boy some clothes. 'What's your name, son?' 'Jim Jarvis,' replied the boy. 'How old are you, Jim?' 'Ten.' 'Have you ever heard of Jesus?'

Jim glanced nervously into the dark corners of the room. His voice dropped to a whisper. 'He's the Pope o' Rome,' he said. Tom was horrified; he leapt to his feet, dragged Jim's chair even closer to the fire, then drew up his own. 'I've a wonderful story to tell you, about a baby born in a place called Bethlehem.'

It was past midnight when Tom finished the story of Jesus. The lad was bright. 'Yeah, them Roman soldiers are just like the policemen in London, ain't they, sir?'

Holding hands, their heads still low against the wind, they set off to find Jim's homeless mates. The boy had said that it was in 'the 'Change', an old-clothes market in a great long shed, off Petticoat Lane. The moon was hidden behind a cloud and, apart from the wind, all was quiet and still in the dark alleys that Jim knew so well.

There was no sound either when they finally entered the ghostly market, full of small, bolted shops. No sound, except the echo of Tom's footsteps. At the far end of the shed, by the wall, Jim removed his stockings. Feeling with his freezing toes for the well-worn grooves, he climbed like a monkey up the ten-foot wall; then through a gap, onto the iron-domed roof of the shed. Using a stick, he helped up his new friend.

And there they were, the homeless boys! With their heads on the higher part of the dome and their feet in the gutter, eleven sleeping boys were huddled together for warmth. Their rags were even worse than Jim's had been, barely covering their bony bodies. The moon came from behind the cloud, revealing their pale, pinched faces. To Tom, it seemed that the hand of God had suddenly pulled aside the curtain which concealed from his view the untold miseries of forlorn child-life on the streets of London.

'Shall I wake them, sir?' Jim said loudly. Tom shook his head. 'Don't let us disturb them.' Tom felt so powerless to help them that he dared not interrupt their sleep. He was already worried about looking after this one little lad, and to wake these eleven, to hear their cries for food and help, was more than he could bear. So taking one last look at their pinched faces, he beckoned Jim to lead the way down.

Tom was deep in thought as they hurried back through the shed. He told himself that he must shelter, feed, clothe and care for this boy. But what about all the other boys like him in London? 'Am I ready at all costs to devote myself to the task of finding these poor destitutes and saving them from a life of misery and crime?'

Chapter Four

The hall clock had struck five and Tom was still trying to sleep after their return. His meeting with Jim Jarvis had shown him the direction of his life. 'My work lies among the poor of London, not China,' he told himself.

Later that day, Tom found lodgings for Jim with one of the neighbours, a missionary lady. He promised to pay for everything. Over the next few nights, Jim helped Tom find sixteen more homeless boys. Tom found them all lodgings and paid all their expenses.

Soon after this, Tom attended one of the special Sunday afternoon services held in the great Agricultural Hall, Islington. Many missionaries were here, as were several notable speakers from abroad. But three speakers failed to arrive, so Tom was asked to talk about his own work. Though he'd taught and preached countless times to groups of poor people, this would be his first actual speech in public and he was nervous before such a large, important audience.

Once he'd begun, though, he forgot his nerves and was soon bringing tears to many eyes. Afterwards, a young woman approached. Squeezed in her palm was a small parcel. 'I'm only a servant-girl, sir, and can't give much, but I've saved all my farthings for the foreign missions. But now I've heard you speak of all those poor children sleeping out, I want to give you the money instead.' This was the first public money that Tom had ever received directly.

Back at home, Tom was thinking hard. The homeless boys couldn't stay in their lodgings for ever. 'If only I had the money to give them all a home together.'

He decided to write more about his work and, in time, his articles in *The Revival* began to stir the consciences of influential people and the money came in to help his work with the poor. And funds were also being boosted by selling photos comparing the past and present conditions of the Ragged School children.

In December 1870, Tom opened a boys' home. He'd rented two large, adjoining terraced houses in Stepney Causeway, a narrow, squalid street. First to arrive were Jim and five friends. They alighted from the hansom cab with Tom then climbed the three steps to the freshly painted black front door. 'The number on the door says 18,' boasted Jim; quite the young scholar now, having joined the Ragged School. Nervously, they followed Mr Barnardo up to one of the five dormitories. A weak sun was shining on newly white-washed walls and on religious pictures and texts. 'Welcome home, boys,' said Tom.

Each night, Tom and Jim trawled the streets and soon the home had twenty-five residents. Following the opening of 18 Stepney Causeway, the donations quickly

doubled. Soon there were sixty residents and
Tom had the dormitories enlarged to make
room for eighty more. He also had workshops
built to teach the boys brush-making and
boot-making so that they could sell their
wares. He already had the hugely profitable
Wood-chopping Brigade, which he'd founded
two years before. And now he started a
uniformed City Messengers' Brigade. The lads
of the Limehouse Shoeblack Brigade were
also proud of their Barnardo uniforms and
badges. Between them, all these hard-working
groups were earning hundreds of pounds and
Tom opened another school, at Salmon Lane.
'Soon it'll be thousands, for the home and for
the schools!' he told himself.

Other boys were learning to be carpenters,
engineers, tailors and bakers. This work was
of use to the home itself, as Tom had no need
to spend money on tradesmen. The lads did
all the housework, too. They made their
beds, cooked and waited at table. And twenty
at a time scrubbed the floor of the schoolroom
upstairs till they were red and it was white.
Under his 'half-time system', all the boys
spent half the day in the school; the other

half learning a trade. But Tom regarded industrial training as more important than schoolwork. By May 1871, five boys from the home had found jobs where they'd be living at their work, so he had vacancies to fill.

He set off before dawn one morning and went to 'the Queen's Shades', an alley by Billingsgate Fish Market which was piled with barrels, crates and boxes.

'A ha'penny for each of you!' Tom shouted. And then he shouted the words again - and again. Eventually, seventy-two scrawny boys emerged from their shelters.

And then, as dawn broke, one more crawled from his barrel. The wizened face was almost hidden by a matted mop of red hair. 'A really ugly-looking little devil!' thought Tom. The boy looked about eight but was probably nearer eleven.

Tom explained his mission to them all and then picked five of the most forlorn-looking lads. As he turned to leave with them, his overcoat sleeve was grabbed. It was the red-haired boy. 'Please take me in, guv'nor,' he murmured. 'I'm sorry,' said Tom, 'we're full up.' The boy sank to his bare knees. 'I

beg you, please take me in.' He scarcely had
the strength to speak. But the chosen five
and, indeed, many of the others looked just
as exhausted. Tom had to be firm. 'I really
am very sorry, son,' he said, patting his head
to try to comfort him. 'But one of my lads is
leaving this day week. I promise you I'll come
for you then at this time.' The boy staggered
to his feet. 'Oh, thank you, sir.' Then, 'I'm
John Somers but everyone calls me Carrots.'

Tom was back at Billingsgate seven days
later but there was no sign of Carrots. 'Where's
Carrots?' he asked. Rubbing a dripping nose
on a dirty sleeve, the biggest boy sniffed,
'Dead as a door-nail.' 'What?' gasped Tom,
'how?' 'Some porters found him in an empty
sugar barrel. Worn out, starving, cold, and
dead.'

The next day, Tom went to the funeral.
'Did poor Carrots love Jesus?' he asked a tiny
lad crying at the graveside. 'Law, sir, we never
hear of Jesus; nor of nothin' good. His
name's only spoken in cussin' and swearin',
which is all we ever hear down here. Can
you take *me* in your 'ome instead of Carrots?'
'Of course, boy,' said Tom, putting an arm

round him. Then, to himself, 'You, child, at least, shall hear something better now. Never again shall I turn a boy away! Never again! I'll leave the hall light on every night so lads will know I have an ever-open door.'

That very afternoon, Tom had a long board fixed above the ground-floor windows of the Stepney home. The painted words said:

NO DESTITUTE BOY

EVER REFUSED

ADMISSION

....

Everyone had heard of Lord Shaftesbury, 'The Friend of the Friendless'. He was the greatest social reformer of the century, and nearly as old as it. An Evangelical himself, he'd met Tom and had encouraged him.

Lord Shaftesbury was still deeply involved with helping the poor and he wanted to know more about the London missionary

NO DESTITUTE BOY EVER REFUSED ADMISSION

33

work. So he invited Tom to tea, along with other mission leaders. After tea, he praised the missionaries for their work and then invited them to speak about it.

Tom's turn finally came. 'I arrived in London six years ago, without a friend and without a farthing, and now I run the largest Ragged School in the capital,' he said. 'I've found vast numbers of children sleeping out! Let me tell you about them. This is the story of Jim Jarvis...'

Tom later claimed that he was the clever fellow who'd told the great Lord Shaftesbury about the vast numbers of outcast children. Barnardo was an inventive story-teller. He said that he'd been the special guest whom everyone had eagerly come to hear. And that Shaftesbury had never realized that there were so many homeless waifs and been horrified.

In reality, His Lordship had been caring for the ragged poor before Barnardo had even been born. In 1848, Shaftesbury had told Parliament that the outcasts 'exceed thirty thousand in London alone!' All those years ago, Shaftesbury had written about regularly

finding 'hundreds shivering, all but naked'.
Few of these would still be alive.

There was much to do - and quickly.
More and more boys were dying, like Carrots.

Chapter Five

It was midnight and Martha's feet were cut and bleeding, her bruised little body half-naked. Her blood dripped onto the steps and glistened in the glow from the fanlight above the door. The frail eleven-year-old hardly had the strength to rap with the knocker. She'd already walked a long way through the alleys and it seemed hours since she'd left the Thames coal-barge.

The matron opened the door. Barnardo was behind her in the hall. 'Please, lady. Please, mister. D'you take in little gels?' Martha was given food and shelter for the night and her wounds tended. Next morning, Tom persuaded a female neighbour to care for her at his expense, until something more permanent could be arranged.

Tom lay awake in his warm, comfortable bed worrying about all the Marthas of this world, freezing, famished and homeless. A home for girls was urgently needed. 'But what do I know about looking after little girls? A wife is the only solution! She'd have to be an Evangelical. But where do I find an Evangelical wife?'

He met her at an Evangelical funeral! He remembered Syrie Elmslie from eighteen months before. She'd invited him to talk to the boys of her own Ragged School in Richmond, Surrey. And now here she was at the funeral of the great Evangelical minister, William Pennefather. 'She's charming, serious and two years younger than me. What more could I want?' thought Tom. Though he'd not yet qualified in medicine, he now insisted on being called 'Doctor' because it made people trust him with their money and with all those young lives. 'The wedding of Doctor Barnardo cheered on by hundreds of little Marthas would be the best-possible advertisement for the girls' home!' thought Tom.

However, although Tom could change the lives of thousands, he could not make a woman do something against her will. Syrie Elmslie actually turned down the great Tom Barnardo!

But Tom Barnardo always lived to fight another day! Picking himself up from this unexpected blow, he finally wore down Syrie's resistance. After all, how could any woman resist his Irish charm? His looks had definitely improved with age; he was handsome and broad-shouldered now. But, to Syrie, far more important than charm and looks were his obvious kindness and his inspiring enthusiasm for the urgent work ahead.

On 17 June 1873, Tom and Syrie were married in the six-thousand-seat Metropolitan Tabernacle in Newington Causeway, south-east London. It was packed with Evangelicals and East Enders; Tom could not have wished for better publicity. His family had been unable to come but his father had sent him a gold watch. And there was a wonderful gift from John Sands, a rich Evangelical solicitor. He gave the young couple the lease of a spacious house among the hayfields and green lanes of Essex. Mossford Lodge, Barkingside, near the small town of Ilford, was theirs to use as a girls' home.

Tom and Syrie moved into the lodge but in October their peace and quiet was shattered. Their first residents, twelve small girls, came to live in the adapted coach-house at the back. 'Mercy!' thought Tom. 'They are so ignorant in mind and stunted in body.'

Soon after, Tom described these 'girl savages' to Shaftesbury. 'One, a girl of only nine, filled a baby's mouth with sand and sat on its face! And yet that child is not really of a cruel nature. There was no murderous intent. There was simply intense curiosity to know what would happen, followed by and by with a feeling of real sorrow when she realized how the poor baby had suffered. Like an untaught savage, she has no imagination; her nature has never been developed; she is incapable of putting herself in another's

40

place. This girl has no parents. She was rescued from the possession of a woman who wandered as a vagabond over England with her.'

But most were the offspring of degraded, vicious women. Tom aimed to train this herd of foul-mouthed, filthy-minded daughters of trollops into a clean, respectable band. A band of kitchen-maids, housemaids, parlour-maids, laundry-maids, dairy-maids and cooks, to meet the great demand for female servants. For once in his life, he had let someone else take control: Syrie. She and her lady volunteers and paid helpers had dressed them all alike in dull uniforms. The girls had been strictly, but kindly, disciplined and were living all together in barrack-type conditions.

A year later, there were three times as many 'savages' to tame. Late one night, Tom passed the dormitory upstairs and overheard a vile conversation. The worst of the girls were teaching the others really bad things. 'Lord forgive me!' he gasped. 'By putting them together like this, I'm concentrating all this evil in one place.' It had been difficult enough for him to get the boys used to a barrack system after the freedom of the streets. With girls like these, it was impossible. 'To mass boys together, with no family influence or habits, is dangerous. To do the same with girls is fatal!' thought Tom. 'A girl needs love, someone to care about her. She needs household duties. What's the use of saying that home is the only place for a woman, while no effort is made to give them an idea of what a home might be?'

Tom had deliberately chosen these girls from the lowest of the low because he wanted to rid London of its 'street women'. As Syrie had said, 'How can we expect to grapple with our greatest social sin so long as girls herd in the lowest lodging-houses?' Yet the great Thomas Barnardo was herding them together here! 'Oh, what will people think of me? It's such a humiliating failure!'

But then, tossing in his bed, Tom had an inspired idea. Cottages! Cottages grouped round a village green. Each cottage run by an unpaid, unmarried Christian lady called 'Mother'. All her 'family' dressed simply - but differently. Girls of all ages: from babies, to girls well into their teens training to be hard-working servants. The day would begin and end with family prayers. He could see small bedrooms, with pretty bed-covers and a looking-glass. He could see the girls in the schoolroom and in the laundry. He could see them being their own servants: chamber-maids, charwomen, nurses, cooks, nannies.

This wonderful vision came to an abrupt end with the sudden yelling of his own new-born baby, William Stuart, but nothing could dislodge this great idea.

In 1876, Tom at last obtained his medical diploma and registered as a medical practitioner. But he was far too busy to earn money as a doctor. Syrie wanted the Barnardos to live well, as befitted their new position. What with her demands and another son, Herbert, to support now, it had become a tremendous strain on Tom, mentally and financially. He thanked God that, two years before, he'd become the owner of a children's magazine that he'd been writing for. He'd changed the title to *The Children's Treasury* and, with his gift for story-telling, it was hugely successful. The magazine and his newspaper articles and appeals were delivering thousands of pounds to the cause.

On 9 July 1876, he opened the first fourteen cottages of the Girls' Village Home, just a nice easy walk from Mossford Lodge, the Barnardo's own house.

Chapter Six

For George, no walk was an easy one. He had no legs. But he could do a hand walk; his arm muscles were amazingly strong. Tom was watching him from the first-floor Board Room window of a rebuilt Stepney Causeway, late on a summer's evening. The boy down there in the large paved yard was actually racing six of his friends who had legs. By a process of peculiar leaps and bounds, George went so fast that he defeated the boys' efforts to catch him. Then he played leap-frog with

them, vaulting over their backs. Another
time, at the swimming-baths, Tom saw
George speeding through the water. 'He's like
a porpoise,' Barnardo told the lads with him.
He remembered that when George had been
admitted to the home, he was a rough,
depressed fellow but now, he was very popular
and always smiling.

Tom always showed a particular tenderness
to all afflicted children. The years had rushed
by; not only had Tom opened 'Ever-Open
Doors' in many parts of the UK but he'd
founded regional homes for the disabled. He
was fatter now and to the disabled children
in Bradford, he was their roly-poly Doctor
with the twirly moustache. One Christmas,
these children saved their pocket money and
sent him a pocket-book and purse.

Mentally handicapped children had a
special place in Tom's heart because his
youngest child, Marjorie, was one of them.
He was always writing about her in letters to
friends. 'Marjorie is sweet. She is just pulling
my chair with a "Daddy, darling, where goes
my book?" Which means, what have I done
with her Sunday picture-book? I devour her

with kisses. I cannot tell you how I love these little bairns, not merely my own but all others, wheresoever and whomsoever they are. So does Marjorie. She is like me in that. She adores children.'

Tom and Syrie had had five sons and two daughters: William Stuart, Herbert, Gwendoline (Queenie), Kenward (Kennie), Thomas (Tom), Cyril and Marjorie. Sadly, baby Tom had not lived long. And both Herbert and Kennie had died of diphtheria, the disease which had nearly ended Barnardo's life all those years before.

Despite all the new homes, by the end of 1892 Tom had also boarded out over two thousand children. He'd placed them with carefully selected Christian foster-parents living in country cottages. The youngsters could feed chickens, pick flowers, play in haystacks and help in the house. He'd always hated putting 'his' children into institutions.

Tom had not restricted his caring empire to the UK. He'd been sending thousands of boys and girls to Canada. They'd come not only from the London slums but those in Liverpool and other large cities and towns.

The older ones went on to become farm labourers or domestic servants. The younger were boarded out with families. The children had first been specially selected and given training in the Barnardo homes. Naturally, the tireless Doctor had been to Canada, too, to visit his children and to sort out any problems.

Tom's first homeless boy, Jim Jarvis, was one of those who'd sailed to Canada. Little pale-faced Jim of the stinking slums had eventually become rosy-cheeked Farmer Jim.

Tom Barnardo had loved Jim and all children. But he was getting old and tired. For nearly forty years, working from before dawn to well past midnight, he'd worn his heart out for them.

Tom Barnardo died on 19 September 1905.

Places to visit

Barnardo's website:
www.barnardos.org.uk

Barnardo's
Tanners Lane, Barkingside,
Ilford, Essex.
Cottages, Barnardo's grave and soon
a Heritage Centre

Stepney Causeway, London
Blue plaque
Site of Barnardo's Boys' Home

Ragged School Museum

Copperfield Road, Bow, London.
Barnardo school -
attend a lesson. East End displays

Bethnal Green Museum of Childhood

Cambridge Heath Road,
Bethnal Green, London.
Costumes, toys, etc.

Medical History Tours
(London and throughout Britain)

Sue Weir, 64 Roupell Street, London SE1 8SS.
(Telephone: 020 7928 0765)

London Museums of Health and
Medicine Group

9a St Thomas Street, London SE1 9RY.
(Telephone: 020 7955 4791)
Education packs, publicity leaflets,
exhibitions, etc.

Old Operating Theatre Museum

9a St Thomas Street, Southwark, London.
Victorian operating theatre housed in
300-year-old herb garret

Royal London Hospital Archives and Museum
St Augustine with St Philip's Church
Newark Street, Stepney.
Former hospital church.
Surgery, nursing, videos, etc.

Florence Nightingale Museum
St Thomas's Hospital,
Lambeth Palace Road, Lambeth, London.
Ward, living-room and slum cottage
re-created

Museum in Docklands
West India Quay,
opposite Canary Wharf, London.
Open from September 2001.
Listed warehouse showing Thames history

Museum of Childhood
High Street, Royal Mile, Edinburgh.
Medicine, books, toys, clothes, etc.

Scotland Street School Museum
Glasgow.
Victorian classroom

Staffordshire County Museum
Shugborough Hall, near Milford.
Schoolroom, kitchen, cab, carriages, etc.
Children at Work Gallery

'How We Lived Then' Museum of Shops
Eastbourne, East Sussex.
Shops, rooms: 100,000+ exhibits collected
over 40 years

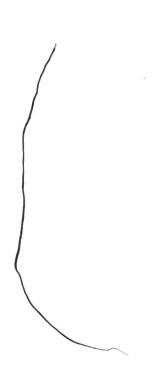